Libraries 7196

LANGLEY PRE-SCHOOL

Babies

Gill Tanner and Tim Wood

Photographs by Maggie Murray
Illustrations by Pat Tourret

A & C Black · London

Here are some of the people you will meet in this book.

The Hart family in 1990

The Cook family in 1960

Lee Hart is the same age as you. His sister Kerry is eight years old. What is Lee's mum called?

This is Lee's mum Linda when she was just nine years old in 1960. She is with her mum and dad, her brother and her baby sister.

The Smith family in 1930

Richard Smith
Lucy Smith
May
Jack and June

The Barker family in 1900

Charles Barker
Alice Barker
Fred
Harry
Lucy
Amy and Adam

This is Lee's granny June when she was just a baby in 1930. Her brother Jack is looking after her.

This is Lee's great grandma Lucy when she was six years old in 1900. Can you see what her sister and her brothers are called?

How many differences can you spot between these two photographs?

One shows a baby in a modern nursery and one shows babies in a nursery one hundred years ago.

This book is about babies.

It will help you find out how looking after babies has changed in the last hundred years.

There are nine mystery objects in this book and you can find out what they are.
They will tell you a lot about people in the past.

This mystery object belonged to the Barker family in 1900.
It is made of wood.
It's just the right size for a baby to sleep in but it isn't a cot.
It has strangely shaped legs.
Can you guess what they were for?
Do you know what this mystery object is called?
Turn the page to find out.

Alice is sewing in the kitchen.
Can you see the mystery object in the picture?
It's a **cradle**.

Alice has just fed baby Adam.
She has put him in the cradle to have a nap.
She rocks the cradle gently
by pushing one of the wooden legs with her foot.
The rocking helps Adam to get to sleep.
The cradle is very old.
Alice slept in it when she was a baby.
What did you sleep in when you were a baby?

Adam Barker used this mystery object in 1900 when he was a baby.
Both parts of it are made of glass.
One of the parts is a bottle.
It is a bit bigger than it is shown here.
The other part is a glass tube.
How do you think the two parts fit together?
Can you guess what went into the bottle?
What do you think this object is?

Turn the page to find out.

Amy is feeding baby Adam.
Can you see the mystery object in the picture?
It's a **feeding bottle** for milk.

Amy filled the feeding bottle with warm milk.
She slid a rubber tube with a teat on the end
over the glass tube.
Then she pushed the glass tube into the top of the bottle.
Baby Adam is drinking the milk through the teat.
Drinking from feeding bottles could make babies ill,
because the parts of the bottles were hard to keep clean.
Can you think why?

This mystery object belonged to the Barkers in 1900.
It's nearly as tall as you are.
The mystery object is mainly made of wood,
but it has some metal parts.
Can you see the wheels?
Have you ever seen anything like it?
What do you think it is?

Turn the page to find out.

The mystery object is a **high chair**.
It could be used in three different ways.

2 Alice has folded the chair to turn it into a low chair on wheels. Alice is lifting a flap in the seat. She is going to put a potty in the hole.

1 Adam is sitting in the high chair eating a rusk.

3 Alice has pulled the chair legs up. Now it is a rocking chair. Adam likes being rocked. It makes him laugh.

This mystery object was used when June Smith
was a baby in 1930.
It is made of metal.
If you were to stand next to the object
it would be level with your tummy.
A big clue is that it has something to do with water.
What do you think it is?

Turn the page to find out.

Baby June is having a bath.
Can you see the mystery object in the picture?
It's a **baby's bath**.

Lucy Smith filled the bath with warm water.
Then she lifted June into the bath.
Lucy is washing June with baby soap.
Have you ever helped to bath a baby?
What was your baby's bath made of?

Lucy Smith used these mystery objects together
when June Smith was a baby.
Two of the mystery objects are made of cloth.
One is towelling and the other is muslin.
If each of these pieces of cloth was unfolded,
it would be bigger than both these pages together.
The third mystery object is made of metal.
You may have seen something like it before.
What do you think these things are?

Turn the page to find out.

Lucy is changing June's nappy.
Can you spot the mystery objects in the picture?
They are **nappies** and a **safety pin**.

First Lucy folded the square nappies into triangles.
She put the thin muslin nappy on first,
so the soft cloth was next to June's skin.
Next she put the towelling nappy
over the muslin nappy.
She is fastening the nappies with the safety pin.
In 1930 there were no disposable nappies.
Lucy washed all the dirty nappies in boiling water.
That way she could use each nappy many times.

Lucy Smith saw this mystery object
when she took June to the baby clinic in 1930.
The bottom part is made of metal.
The base would cover one page of this book.
What do you think the numbers show?
Look carefully, you may spot a big clue.
The top part is made of wicker and shaped like a tray.
Have you ever seen anything like it?
What do you think it is?

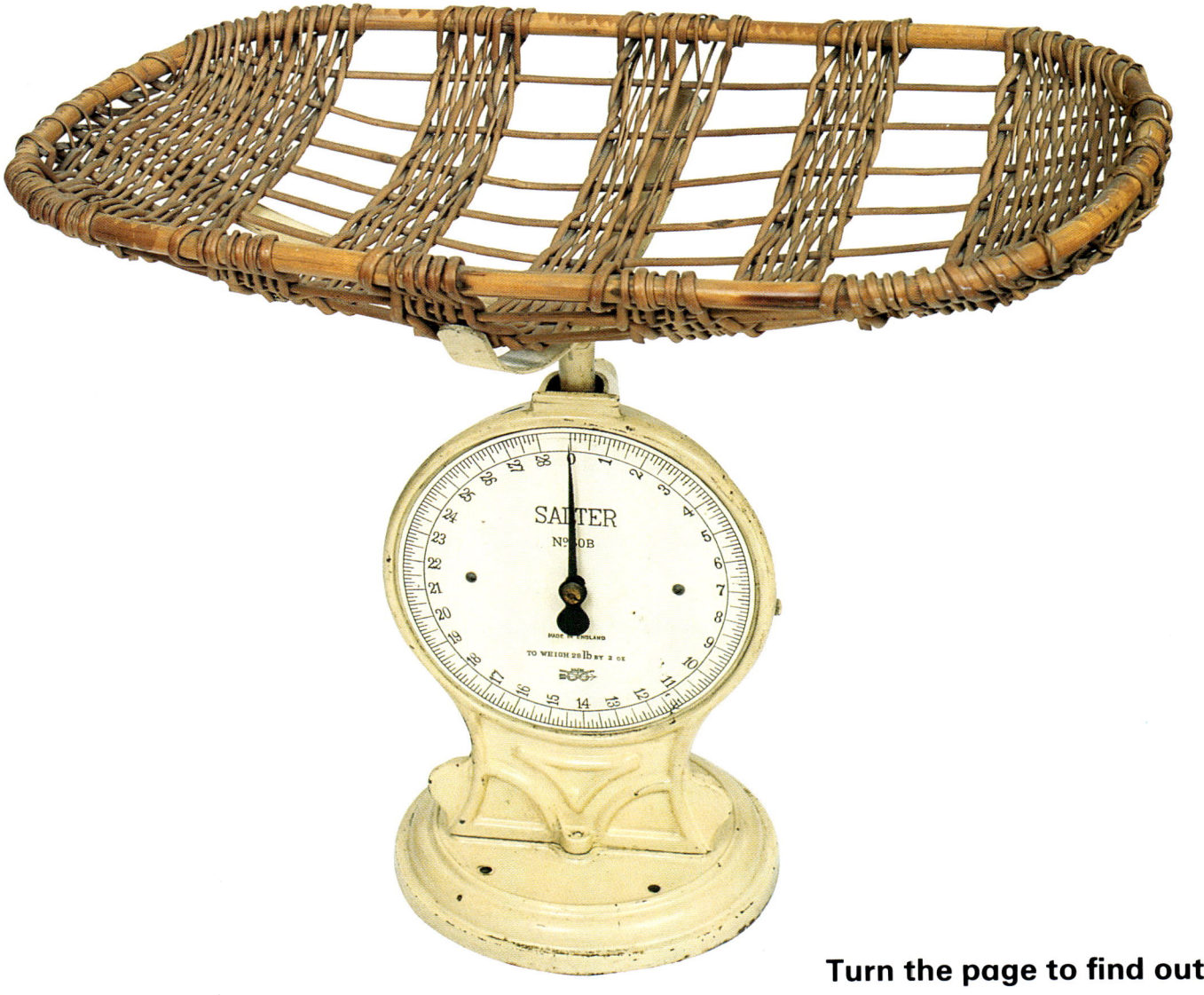

Turn the page to find out.

Lucy Smith is at the baby clinic.
Can you spot the mystery object?
It's a **baby scales**.
A nurse weighs June on the baby scales.
She writes down June's weight on a record card,
which shows how well June is growing.

When June has been weighed,
Lucy will take her to the doctor for an injection.
The injection is a vaccination
which will stop June catching a disease called smallpox.
Did you have a vaccination when you were a baby?

The Cook family used this mystery object
when Susan was a baby in 1960.
It is about the same size
as the mystery object on page five.
It is made of plastic material
stretched over wooden boards.
It has handles, and a hood which goes up and down.
What do you think it is?

Turn the page to find out.

The Cook family are going shopping.
Can you see the mystery object in the picture?
It's a **carry cot**.

When the family goes out in the car,
Susan sleeps on the back seat in the carry cot.
June carries the cot by its handles.
The carry cot is very useful
and the plastic material is easy to clean.
June can fit the carry cot into a frame with wheels
to turn it into a pram.
She can use the carry cot as a cradle as well.

This mystery object is made of nylon
with metal buckles.
Stretched out, it would fit right across this open book.
It could be used in lots of different ways
to keep a baby safe.
What do you think it is?

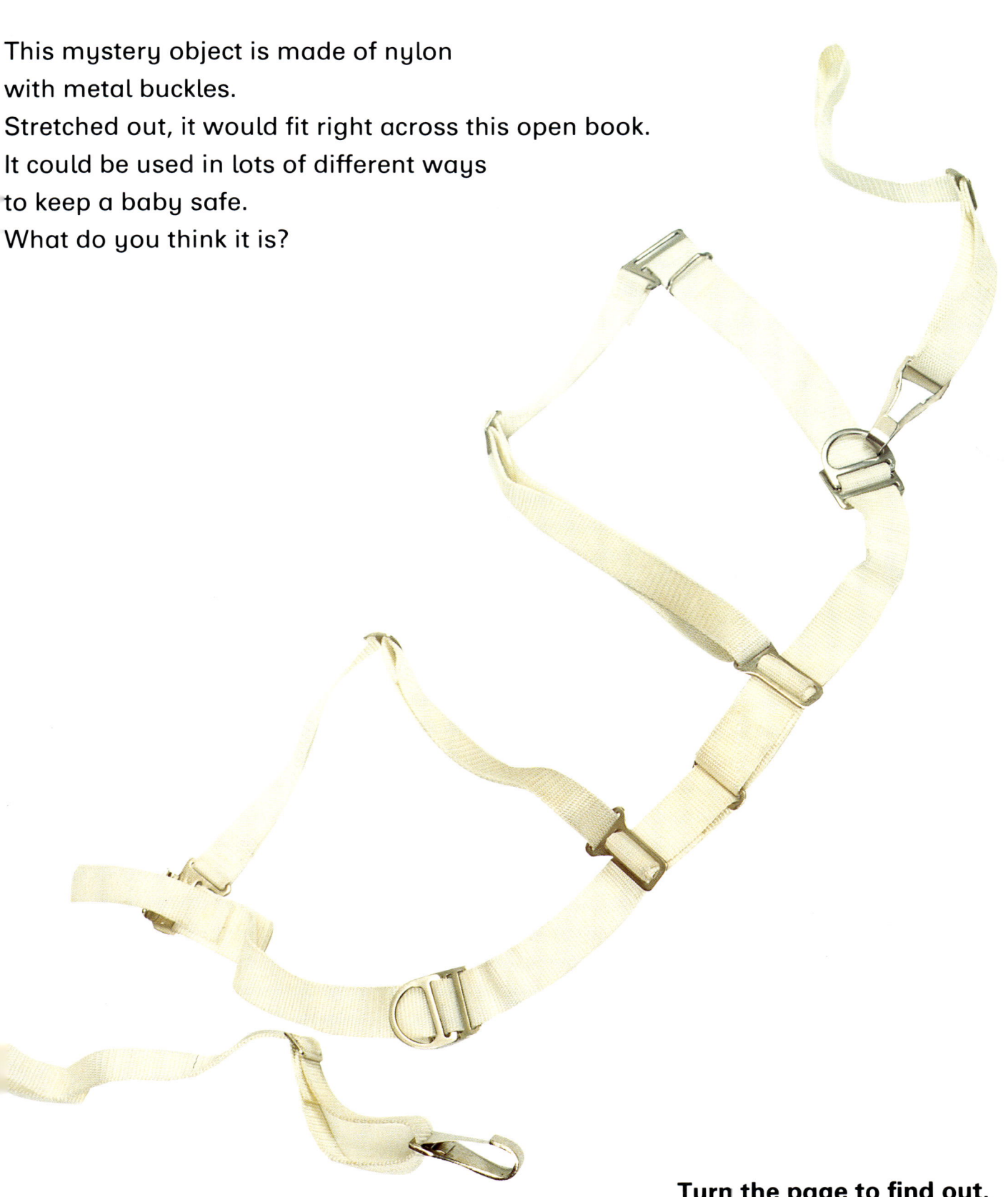

Turn the page to find out.

The Cooks are in the supermarket.
Can you see the mystery object in the picture?
It's a **baby's harness**.

In 1960 June and David Cook used the harness
when they went out.
It kept baby Susan close to them
and helped her to walk without falling.
June put Susan's arms through the loops
and clipped the straps together behind Susan's back.
June steadies Susan with reins clipped to the harness.
Did you ever walk with a harness and reins?

Now that you know a bit more about babies
and how bringing them up has changed
over the last one hundred years,
see if you can guess what
this mystery object is.

It belonged to baby Adam Barker in 1900
when the object was already very old.
It is about the same size as it is shown on this page.
The handle is made of coral.
The rest is made of silver.
What do you think it is?

You will find the answer on page 24.

Time-line

These pages show you the objects in this book and the objects we use for bringing up babies nowadays.

1900
The Barker family

1930
The Smith family

1960
The Cook family

1990
The Hart family

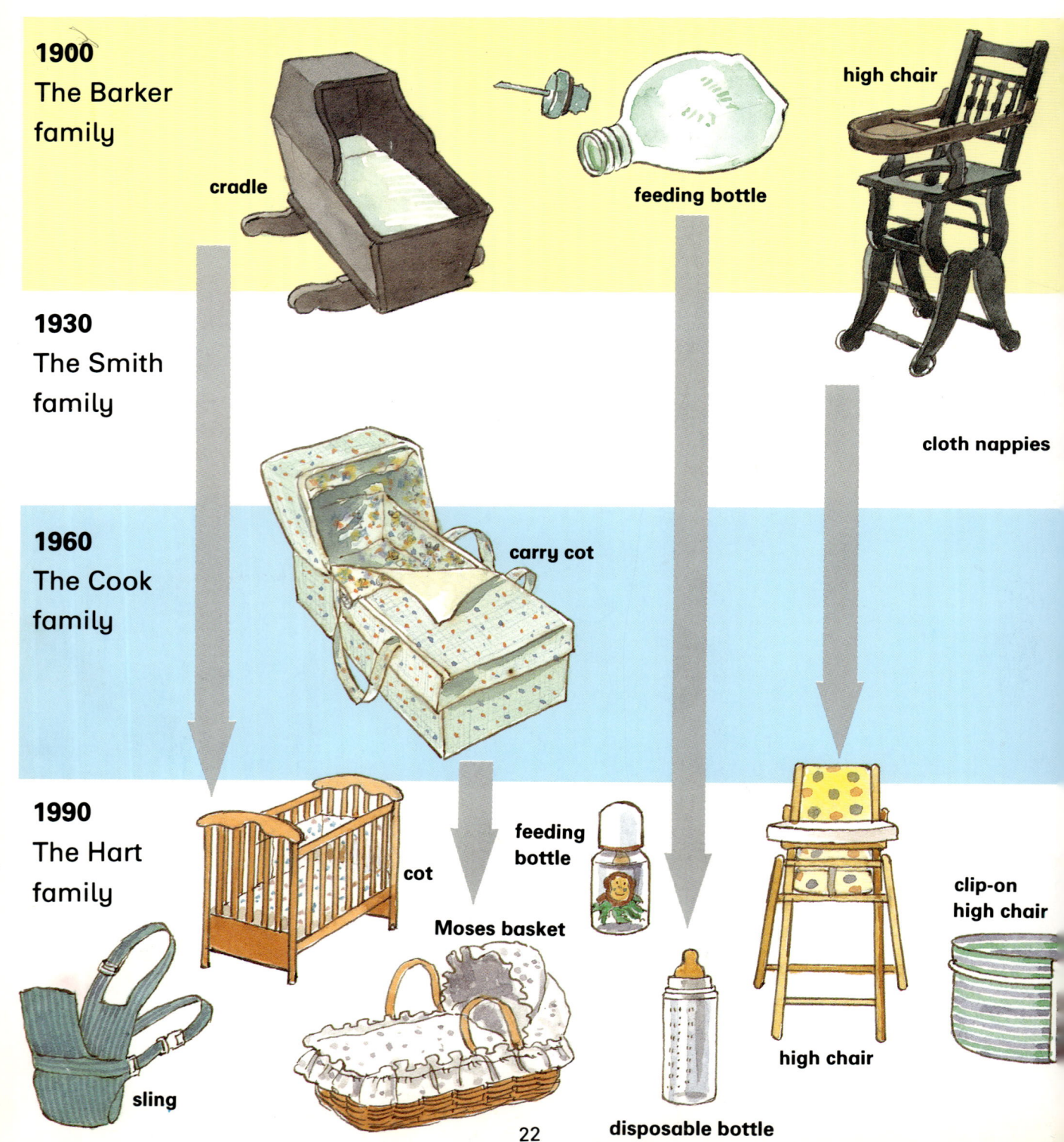

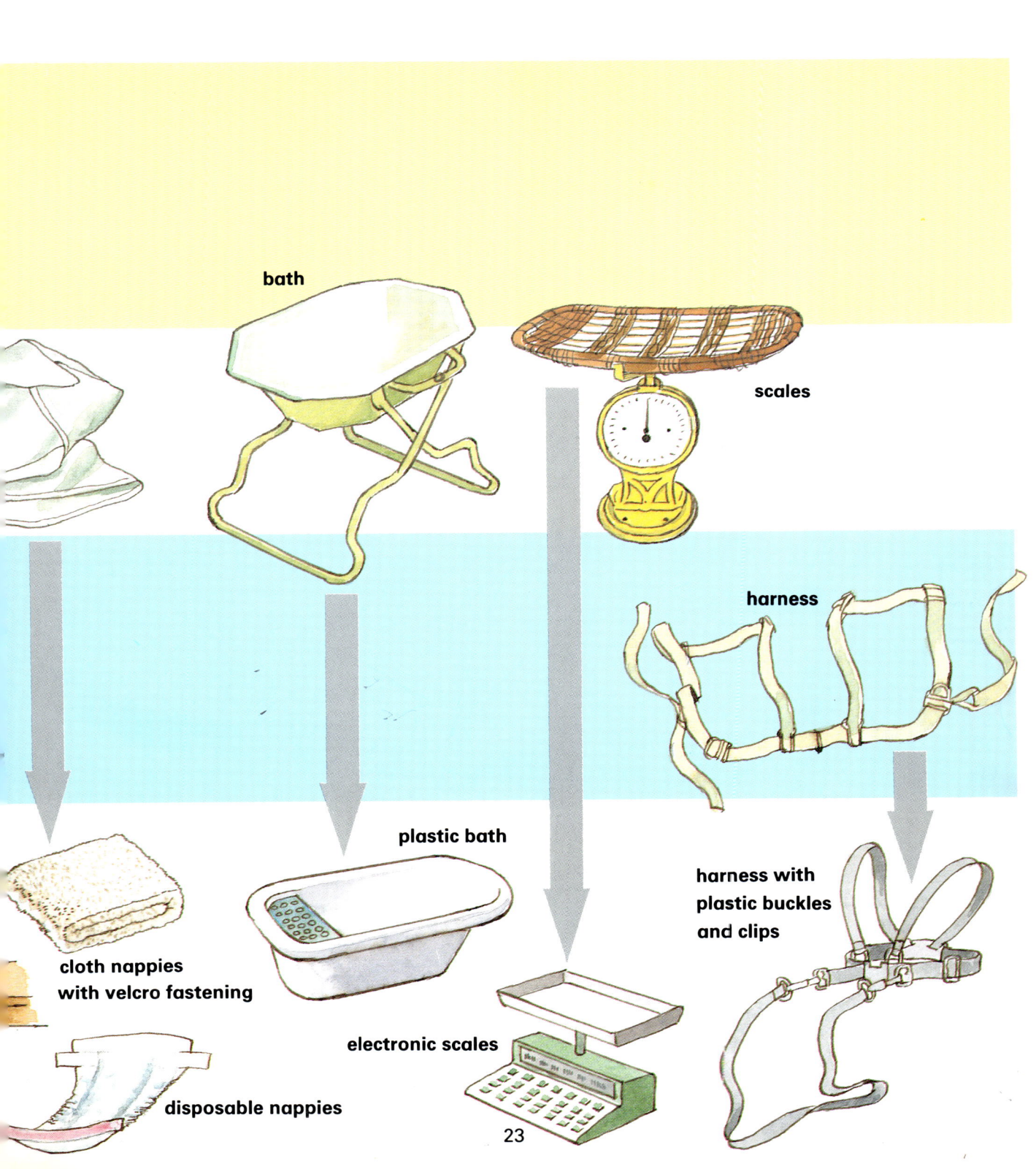

Index

Bb baby's bath *12, 23*
baby clinic *15, 16*
baby's harness *20, 23*
baby scales *16, 23*
Barker family *5–10, 21*
Cc carry cot *18, 22*
cloth *13, 14*
Cook family *17, 18, 20*
cot *5*
cradle *6, 18, 22*
Ff feeding bottle *8, 22*
Gg glass *7, 8*
Hh high chair *10, 22*
Mm metal *9, 11, 13, 15, 19*
milk *8*
Nn nappies *14, 23*
nylon *19*
Pp plastic *17, 18*
potty *10*
pram *18*
Rr record card *16*
reins *20, 23*
rubber *8*
Ss safety pin *14, 23*
smallpox *16*
Smith family *11–16*
Vv vaccination *16*
Ww water *11, 12*
wheels *9, 10*
wicker *15*
wood *5, 6, 9, 17*

The **mystery object** on page 21 is a **baby's teething rattle**. It is over 200 years old. It has bells on the sides and a whistle at one end. Coral was thought to bring good luck. Rattles like this were often given as Christening presents.

For parents and teachers
More about the objects and pictures in this book

Pages 5/6 Cradles similar in design and materials to the one shown have been in use for hundreds, if not thousands of years. The hood is designed to protect the baby from strong light and draughts.

Pages 7/8 Breast feeding became less popular in Victorian times. Richer mothers employed wet nurses. 'Propped' feeding as shown in the picture was common at this time although it was dangerous because of the risk of choking. Bottle-fed babies were rarely cuddled. The type of bottle shown was in common use. It was impossible to clean properly and was a breeding ground for germs. Babies were generally fed with untreated cows' milk or one of the many brands of baby milk which were not very nourishing and often carried diseases. By about 1910 this type of bottle had been replaced by much safer, boat-shaped bottles such as the Allenbury Feeder.

Pages 9/10 The seat flap and potty are missing from the chair in the photograph.

Pages 11/12 The bath is painted and can be lifted out of its folding stand.

Pages 13/14 Re-usable nappies like these are now thought to have environmental advantages over disposable nappies. The terry towelling nappy is much more absorbent than the muslin nappy, but could chafe, especially when wet. Nappies had to be boiled until the invention of cold-water sterilizing products in the 1960s.

Pages 15/16 Baby clinics developed after 1918. Child health care became a compulsory subject for trainee doctors and midwives in 1919.

Pages 17/18 Carry cots were widely used in the 1960s both indoors and outdoors as cradles, cots, prams and in the car.

Pages 19/20 Before the introduction of nylon straps in the 1960s baby harnesses and reins were made of leather.

Things to do

History Mysteries will provide an excellent starting point for all kinds of history work. There are lots of general ideas which can be drawn out of the pictures, particularly in relation to the way bringing up babies, clothes, family size and lifestyles have changed in the last 100 years. Below are some starting points and ideas for follow-up activities.

1 Work on families and family trees can be developed from the family on pages 2/3, bearing in mind that many children do not come from two-parent, nuclear families. There are many ways of bringing in children's own experiences and linking these to their own family histories.

2 Find out more about caring for babies in the past from a variety of sources, including books, interviews with older people in the community, museums and manufacturers' information. Bringing up babies wasn't the same for everyone. Why not?

3 There is one object which is in one picture of the 1900s, one picture of the 1930s, and one picture of the 1960s. Can you find it?

4 Arrange a field trip to a museum of childhood such as the Bethnal Green Museum of Childhood in London or the Museum of Childhood in Edinburgh.

5 Look at the difference between the photographs and the illustrations in this book. What different kinds of things can they tell you?

6 Make your own collection of baby objects or pictures. You can build up an archive or school museum over several years by encouraging children to bring in old objects, collecting unwanted items from parents, collecting from junk shops and jumble sales. You may also be able to borrow handling collections from your local museum or library service.

7 Encouraging the children to look at the objects is a useful start, but they will get more out of this if you organise some practical activities which help to develop their powers of observation. These might include drawing the objects, describing an object to another child who must then pick out the object from the collection, or writing descriptions of the objects for labels or for catalogue cards.

8 Encourage the children to answer questions. What do the objects look and feel like? What are they made of? What makes them work? How old are they? How could you find out more about them?

9 What do the objects tell us about the people who used them? Children might do some writing, drawing or role play, imagining themselves as the owners of different objects.

10 Children might find a mystery object in their own house or school for the others to draw, write about and identify. Children can compare the objects in the book with objects in their own homes or school.

11 If you have an exhibition, try pairing old objects with their nearest modern counterparts. Talk about each pair. Some useful questions might be: How can you tell which is older? Which objects have changed most over time? Why? Can you test how well the objects work?

12 Make a time-line using your objects. You might find the time-line at the back of this book useful. You could include pictures in your time-line and other markers to help the children gain a sense of chronology. Use your time-line to bring out the elements of *change* (eg. the growth of knowledge about baby care and child development; the introduction of a national health service; how improvements in hygiene, medical knowledge, and facilities in the home have made bringing up baby much easier; the greater involvement of fathers in childcare and increasing emphasis on the value of play) and *continuity* (eg. how people have always had babies; the need to feed, wash, change and transport them).

History Mysteries

First published 1994
A & C Black (Publishers) Limited
35 Bedford Row, London WC1R 4JH

ISBN 0-7136-3801-X
© 1994 A & C Black (Publishers) Limited

A CIP catalogue record for this book is available
from the British Library.

Acknowledgements

The authors and publishers would like to thank Suella Postles and the staff of Brewhouse Yard Museum, Nottingham; Mrs Tanner's Tangible History; Vina Cooke's Museum of Dolls and Bygone Childhood, Cromwell, Near Newark, Notts.

All photographs by Maggie Murray

Apart from any fair dealing for the purposes of research or private study, or criticism or review, as permitted under the Copyright Designs and Patents Act, 1988, this publication may be reproduced, stored or transmitted, in any form, or by any means, only with the prior permission in writing of the publishers, or, in the case of reprographic reproduction in accordance with the terms of licences issued by the Copyright Licensing Agency. Inquiries concerning reproduction outside those terms should be sent to the publishers at the above named address.

Filmset by Rowland Phototypesetting Limited, Bury St Edmunds, Suffolk
Printed and bound in Italy by L.E.G.O.